Murder in Southwest Baltimore

Joe Roy Metheny

J.R. Brand

DEDICATION

As always, my books are dedicated to my Mom in heaven. She's gone but not forgotten! I love you forever and always Mom!
.

"We serial killers are your sons, we are your husbands, we are everywhere. And there will be more of your children dead tomorrow." **Ted Bundy**

CONTENTS

ACKNOWLEDGMENTS

While it is true that an author is the one who develops a story and puts it on "paper", the reality is that it takes many people to bring a book to life, and any author who does not readily admit this is vain and full of his or her self. In my case, there were a number of individuals involved – far too many to list in this section, so I will simply say thank you to those of you who helped me with this one!

.

These children who come to you with their knives, they're your children. I didn't teach them, you did." **Charles Manson**

1 - INTRODUCTION

This book has had many iterations over the two years prior to being actually published. Ultimately, I decided to settle on simply presenting the facts as I have learned them. In some areas of the book, details are sketchy, at best. I contacted many people in an effort to bring this book to life. All but one person opted to not be involved in its creation. The only person in fact that responded, was the serial killer himself, and he wanted to be paid when I offered him the opportunity to tell his story. I refuse to allow him to profit off his crimes, so I never sent him anything, but he did return a letter giving a brief overview of what he had done over a period of 2 years.

"I was born with the devil in me. I could not help the fact that I was a murderer, no more than the poet can help the inspiration to sing..I was born with the evil one standing as my sponsor beside the bed where I was ushered into the world, and he has been with me since. " – **H.H. Holmes**

2 – JOE ROY METHENY

Joe Roy Metheny was by all accounts, "a nice guy". He was affectionately known as "Tiny" to those that he counted among his friends and acquaintances. Sure, he could get angry at times as people often will. Perhaps he had even been involved in the occasional barroom brawl as people sometimes do when there is a large number of people gathered into one place and alcohol is involved. Still, there is not a single person who would have ever believed in their heart of hearts that Tiny was capable of killing anyone.

Joe was born on March 2, 1955 in Baltimore, Maryland, but his family had moved to the area from Terra Alta, West Virginia prior to his birth in order to seek a better life. Even in the 1950's, the job market was scarce in Preston County West Virginia, and let's face it, it takes money to live, so his mom and dad packed the family up and came to the Baltimore area looking for work. They ended up settling in Essex, on the East side of Baltimore City, across the Baltimore County line.

Sometime after Joe's second birthday, his parents moved the family back to Terra Alta, WV where they would remain until Joe's father was killed in a car accident when Joe was just six years old. Not knowing what else to do, Jean Metheny moved her family back to the Essex area so that she could find work to support them. There certainly was not much in the way of work in Preston County, even after all that time had passed. In Baltimore, Jean found work as a barmaid, waitress and even as an attendant on lunch trucks at various times.

Jean did the best that she could to support the family. "There was never a lot of money, but there was always food and a roof over our heads. It was a good life," she had been known to say.

Joe saw things a little differently though. Later, after his eventual arrest and confession to a number of murders, he would claim that he was abused as a child and shuffled from one house to another. At one point, he had told his attorney that his mother was dead. This was of course, later proven false, after one enterprising reporter did a little digging and found Joe's mom, Jean Metheny still alive and well in Markleysburg, Pennsylvania, a small town located less than 30 miles from Terra Alta.

Joe stopped going to school when he was in the eighth grade. It's not that he was stupid or couldn't do the work. He was a bright kid and could do the work easily enough, but he had his own mind and was going to do what he damn well pleased.

Once Metheny turned eighteen years old, he realized that he had to do something to make a living and he joined the Army. His three year hitch in the Army saw him earning his GED certificate and studying physics for a year and a half before being honorably discharged.

Later on, after his arrest, he told his lawyer that he had spent time in Vietnam, but his mother contradicted that and said that he had in fact been stationed in Germany and to her knowledge had never gone to Vietnam. Another of many lies told by Joe, probably in order to gain the sympathy of his lawyer and perhaps the court as well.

When Joe got out of the Army, he returned to the Baltimore area and started working to support himself. It was about that same time that he involved himself in the Baltimore drug scene.

At some point, he lived in a house at 2103 Hollins Ferry Road in between Washington Boulevard and Waterview Ave. This house is situated between Morrell Park in Baltimore City and Westport. This will be the house that he had presumably lived in when his common-law wife left him, taking their son with her. In any case, by 1988, he had begun working for the Joe Stein and Son Pallet Company, located on James Street, just off Caton Avenue in Baltimore, near Halethorpe/Arbutus. He had told people that he was a truck driver, however, what he had actually done there was to operate a forklift.

Like most other companies of that nature, Joe had been expected to work overtime at peak times in order that the company could get their orders completed. On one such day Joe had worked the required overtime, finally getting home that night, tired and hungry. When he got to the house, his "ol lady" had disappeared with his kid and everything that they owned as well. "I didn't care that the bitch left," he said. "I would have paid her to leave, but when she left, she took my son and she wasn't even capable of taking care of herself. She was more worried about the drugs than she was the kid. All she would have had to do was take him to my mother's house and she could have stayed gone for all I cared."

Metheny would claim that this was his "breaking point", a point in time when all serial killers begin to act out their fantasies rather than just think about them. More from Joe:

"After about six months, I found out that she moved in with some asshole over on the east side of town. I now had a mission in life. To find that dirty bitch and the motherfucker that she left with so that I could get my kid back. My son. My blood. She was a crack-addicted whore and I couldn't care less if that motherfucker lived or died, my son was a different story though."

"It wasn't too much longer after I found out all of that shit, that I heard they were over in tent city getting' high. I went over to have a look for myself. By that time, I had heard that he was pimping her stupid ass out on the streets so that they could get money for drugs. I also learned that they had been popped for drugs and that my son was now in foster care. I didn't have a snowball's chance in hell of getting him back by then because I didn't have a stable house to bring him to, and besides, by then I had had a criminal record and there was no way he was going to get to come live with me. If I had gotten him though, things might have turned out differently. As it was, they had they drug charges as well as child abuse and neglect."

On the streets, word has a way of getting around when things are going on. All it takes is a couple of questions here and there. Most of the time the word on the streets is exaggerated, but there is almost always some ring of truth to it or the rumors would not have started to begin with.

"I took it upon myself to find these two assholes and make them pay for what they had done to my boy. I had every intention of killing them two motherfuckers. When I found out that they had been going to tent city, I went looking for them."

On Patapsco Avenue in Southwest Baltimore, there is a bridge that crosses the Patapsco River. Under this bridge there exists a completely different world, separate and apart from the rest of society. In this world, the homeless exist on the fringes of society. There is a lawlessness that most everyday citizens rarely glimpse, if they see it at all.

In the case of this particular "community", there was a lot of fighting going on between two different camps at this particular time, drugs were prevalent, and people were being robbed of what little they had; none of it was ever reported to the police.

"When I got under the bridge and made it to the homeless camp, I didn't find my ex-ol' lady or her asshole boyfriend. I did find two of the homeless motherfucker's that they had been getting high with though. These two assholes were asleep on a stinking old mattress that was under the bridge. I woke the motherfuckers up by kicking at them and yelling for them to get the fuck up. When they finally did, I started asking about my ol' lady. They admitted that they had been getting high with both of the motherfuckers. When I left from under the bridge, those two motherfuckers were back on the mattress, only now they were dead. I knocked 'em both out and before I left the camp, I found an ax and hacked the motherfuckers up with it. I was that fuckin' mad. Before I left though, I cleaned out their pockets but ended up with less than twenty bucks. I threw some old bushes and a ratty blanket that I found on top of the bodies and got the hell out of there." Some other asshole would get blamed but not charged for killing them. When it was all said and done, I admitted to being the one that killed them.

3 – WHAT IS A SERIAL KILLER?

Before you move further along and start reading the story, it's important that you understand exactly what a serial killer is. By and large, the average person does not know exactly what a serial killer is, though they know that he or she kills multiple people for various reasons that they may not fully understand.

A true serial killer is a psychopath. He has no feeling or compassion for anyone other than himself, mamking it easier for him to separate himself from his or her crimes. Most serial killers will have some sort of breaking point in their lives. A point where they seem to throw in the towel and act out the ways that they do.

From where does the urge that a serial killer gets to kill come? It seems that these urges are so powerful, that the serial killer has little power to overcome them and they have to act out. The question on the minds of the many who study serial crime is whether the urges are genetic, hormonal or if it comes from the culture, in which we live.

Another question that arises is whether the serial killer has any control over their desire to commit these heinous acts or not. The fact is, that in general we all experience rage at some point in our lives, yet we stop at a certain point before causing harm to others. Something inside of us keeps that sort of rage in check.

Serial killers come up with any number of excuses for their behavior. Ted Bundy has publicly stated that pornography and detective magazines were the catalyst for his fantasies. Hebert Mullin and David Berkowitz claimed it was the voices in their heads. In the case of Berkowitz, the voice was that of a dog. Jeffrey Dahmer used to tell doctors that there was something "missing" inside of him. The average person will believe that these people must be insane and easy to pick out of a crowd, because a "normal" person simply would not kill another human being because they liked it and found it to be pleasurable.

What is the definition of a serial killer though? According to the FBI, a serial killer will have a minimum of two victims whom they have killed, with a period in between the murders termed as a "cooling off" period. Other sources say that there should be three victims. The victim of the serial killer is usually a stranger.

In nearly every case, the murder will be a reflection of the serial killer's need to dominate his victim(s) in a sadistic manner. A serial killer will rarely rob his victim, although there are a few documented cases where robbery was in fact the motive. The true motivation behind the murder however is generally psychological in nature with the killer feeling the need to dominate. In most cases, the victims will be symbolic to the serial killer in some way and the method of which he kills those victims may reveal this symbol to investigators.

A serial killer will also usually leave some sort of signature to the crime. For instance, with Gary Ray Bowles, the subject of my second book, and a person who is actively working with me to complete it, would stuff something into the mouth of his victims like a rag, or filling the mouth full of dirt. Finally, while there are a few exceptions, a serial killer will usually choose his victims from a pool of people who live on the fringes of society such as prostitutes or runaways.

Statistically speaking, the average serial killer is going to be a white male who comes from a middle-class or lower background, though he can come from any class of society. He will usually be in the twenties to thirties age range. Of this group, many of have been physically or emotionally abused by their parents. In many cases both types of abuse is present. When looking deeper, we find that some of these people have been adopted.

The Macdonald Triad shows us that these serial killers have been found to be pyromaniacs when they were young, they had been torturing or killing small animals and they regularly wet the bed accidentally beyond the age of five. We will look at the triad in more detail later on in this chapter.

Over the years, as we learn more about these behaviors, we find that the criteria are not etched in stone. Far from it in fact, because now we know that the serial killer is NOT always a white male, as we once believed. There are plenty of examples available showing that other races represent the serial killer field as well. Perhaps not as often as the white man, but they are there just the same. Likewise, women are not immune from becoming serial killers either – case in point: Aileen Wournos who was a prostitute that murdered her "dates" and robbed them.

It was also once believed that the typical serial killer was of average or below in the intelligence department. That is not the case either. For example, H.H. Holmes was a doctor who murdered, and there are other examples as well that can show that intelligence has nothing, or at least very little, to do with serial murder.

In our society, we believe that we can easily spot when someone is "crazy" or psychotic. Think about what we do on a daily basis. I mean, when we walk down the street, we avoid mentally ill and handicapped people, unless of course we know them. We just go about our routine; thinking in our minds that we need to stay away from "that one" and everything will be fine.

The simple truth is that the people we need to be avoiding is the one that is a well-dressed individual who speaks to us politely and blends in with the rest of society, because I'm here to tell you friends, those are the people you need to watch out for. The serial killers that we see throughout history do not look like what the average person thinks they look like. A psychopath makes it his priority to fit in to the rest of the world. He must work to blend in, so that he can carry on with his acts of violence. Otherwise, he would be caught very quickly. That is how Ted Bundy and Gary Ridgway carried on for as long as they did before they were captured. As one attorney has said, "Dress him in a suit and tie, and he looks like 10 other people." These people work to hide behind a façade of normalcy, to make it *appear* as if they were just like you and I.

Serial killers are unable to feel anything for anyone else. They have no empathy for anyone, and that enables them to carry on with their crimes.

Because they are unable to feel this empathy, they must watch what is going on around them, and they emulate what others are doing in order to bring themselves across to others as being "normal."

One serial killer has been known to say that a serial killer is an actor who is simply "playing a part." In this case, their role is the serial killer, who is able to kill and then go back to what appears to be a normal everyday life for the average guy. Everything that they do is part of their act. For instance, when in court, Ted Bundy said, "Today my role is that of an attorney." This reiterates what other serial killers have said about their lives being a role that they play. A serial killer is able to look at his victims as being objects rather than human beings. Ted Bundy was easily able to slip into various roles with his most prominent role probably being the fact that he was successfully able to present himself as a rape crisis counselor.

The favorite role for a serial killer to play it seems, is that of a person who is in authority. For instance, John Wayne Gacy was very active in business and society in general. He had even become a member of the civic group the "Jaycees". Others like the Hillside Stranglers, Angelo Buono and Kenneth Bianci liked to take on the role of a police officer. In a nutshell and to be quite blunt about it, the serial killer works very hard at putting across an air of sanity and intelligence until he gets caught, and then he wants people to believe that he is in fact, insane. At the time of capture, serial killers will feign multiple personalities, schizophrenia and anything else that they can think of to make them appear to be "crazy". In reality however, a serial killer knows exactly what he is doing and he is well aware of the consequences when he is caught. He just feels nothing for the victims. Even when they do express remorse, and they "work with authorities", they are still acting in their role.

Even up to now, FBI agents work to get inside the mind of the serial killer. We need to do this of course, because we are looking for answers that will help to catch serial killers in the future. The explanations that they get from the serial killers include child abuse early in life, genetic reasons, brain injuries and exposure to traumatic events among other things.

What makes things scary is that the majority of people in the world have been exposed to at least one of these things in their lives. That said, it still leaves us open to the question of what sets a serial killer apart from the rest of the human population? As a species, we believe that we have the ability to stop ourselves from committing heinous acts, regardless of how angry we may become. We believe that there is something built in to us that stops us from taking out our aggression on others *in most cases*.

Serial killer Dennis Nilsen said that he was incapable of stopping his murderous spree. Does that mean that the so-called "moral safety latch" is missing from the serial killer? There is no doubt that the mind of the serial killer is seriously sick. It is scary to think about, but it would seem that the number of serial killers out there in the world continues to grow. Does it mean that the serial killer has some sort of disease that needs to be treated? If so, what could possibly be the cure to put an end to it?

It is clear that some serial killers are fascinated by sadistic violence from the time that they are very young. It is for that reason that one of the first places we look, as a society for the explanation as to why a person does what he does is his early family life and upbringing. We want to believe that something traumatic must have happened to the serial killer when he was a child that caused him to turn out to be a murderer. That would seem plausible until you take a look at the case of Jeffrey Dahmer. The fact of the matter is however, that Dahmer had what most people would believe to be the ideal upbringing.

When looking at child abuse, in many cases unfortunately, the child abuse by a parent is barbaric. It seems that there is no wonder a child grows up to become a serial killer, acting out against the wrongs that he has experienced in life. A serial killer will often relay stories of horrifying physical abuse, torture and mayhem. While it is true that some of the stories are likely exaggerated in order to gain sympathy from the listener, there are some cases where witnesses have verified the stories.

Even when you encounter a family that appears to be the "perfect family" on the outside, behind closed doors it is a different story. In situations like this, a child will learn how to develop a Jekyll and Hyde existence, all sweet and lovable on the outside but a murderous monster within. At the same time however, we have to look at the many children who have suffered the same traumas in life but have gone on to lead healthy and productive lives. Therefore, we have to realize that while child abuse can be *linked* to a serial killer, it is not the catalyst that triggers the murderous feelings.

In the past, it was believed that when a parent was harsh on his or her children, it would make them stronger and able to go through their adult life more easily. We have since learned however, that being harsh on a child in such a manner can often lead to disastrous results. The fact is if there is not proper bonding between a child and his parents, he will often go through life unable to establish meaningful relationships with anyone. When children are isolated like this, they develop a fantasy world, a world in which they are in control and can alter the outcome of any situation to suit them. More often than not, in situations like this the blame is placed on the mother's shoulders. Whether this is fair or not is still an open question.

Everything seems to begin or end with a serial killer's mother in most cases, however. For instance, Ed Kemper ended his killing spree by killing his mother while people like Henry Lee Lucas started with killing their mothers. Everything seems to hinge on the fact that a serial killer has an unusual relationship in some way with his mother. It would seem that the murderer is still dominated in some way by his mom. People often dismiss these people as "momma's boys". Who knows? Maybe we just find it more comfortable to be able to blame someone for the fact that a person turned into a serial killer.

There are some cases however where the blame CAN be placed on mom's shoulders. Look at Ed Gein. His mother pounded into his head all of his life that women were dirty and sinful. She emphatically told him that he needed to stay away from them because they would only cause him to catch diseases. You will remember Ed Gein, even if you have never heard of him; he was the inspiration for Hitchcock's movie "Psycho". Gein, while he only killed two women that we know of, was more infamous for digging up dead bodies so that he could retrieve the skin to make his "mother suit". He also used the tops of skulls as bowls and ashtrays among other things. He made it through life without getting any sexually transmitted diseases, but his brain at some point definitely became diseased in the process.

In another instance, Kenneth Bianci, one of the "Hillside Stranglers" was adopted. His adoptive mother was very over-protective of him. So much so, that he once accidentally wet himself, so she took him to a doctor to have his genitals examined to see what might be "wrong" with him. There were evidently protective agencies involved at some point, because there were medical notes that Bianci's mother was "deeply disturbed", "dissatisfied", and "overly protective". Bianci had become extremely dependent on his mother while at the same time being extremely hostile toward her.

Some serial killers blame the fact that they turned out as they did because their mother was "loose". For instance, Bobby Jo Long killed women because he believed them all to be whores. Perhaps "mom" had overstepped too much, exposing her child to inappropriate sexual behavior. In long's case, it seemed his mother would have sex with her partners in the same room that he slept in up until he was about 13-years-old. So perhaps there is something to blaming mom in some cases.

We have now sufficiently taken care of blaming mom for the way her serial killer son turned out, (but let us not forget the occasional daughter); let us look at where dad fits into the picture. In the family tree of the serial killer, an unusually sadistic father will usually pop up. In the case of John Wayne Gacy it does. Gacy went through life with his father calling him a sissy, queer, faggot, failure and anything else that he could come up with at the time. Gacy's father was a violent alcoholic who beat his mother and shot his son John's beloved dog in order to punish him. Gacy's M.O. would be to encourage victims to stay brave while he was killing them. He killed it seems, to reassure himself that he was indeed masculine, and not the way his father described him.

With Jeffrey Dahmer, it was different though. Dahmer was not exposed to the abuses that you hear most serial killers talking about occurring early in their lives. By all accounts, Dahmer had a normal and healthy childhood, so what was it that drove him to kill? Dahmer's father, Lionel, believes it happened when Dahmer was still in his mother's womb. Lionel described his wife as being full of hysteria and psychosomatic illness during her pregnancy, which caused Jeffrey to turn out as he did. The elder Dahmer said that his wife Joyce had a difficult pregnancy with Jeff and he believes it was a "biological rejection" that turned him into a killer.

There are some who have wondered whether adoption was a factor in a child growing into a serial killer. Perish the thought because that simply is not the case. There is a possibility of the adopted child going on to meet his biological parents and being hurt because he felt rejected for a second time; the first of course being when he learned that he was given up for adoption to begin with. Look at the case of David Berkowitz, AKA "The Son of Sam". He had learned that he was adopted and said that at times he felt rejected because his "real" parents did not want him. He then learned who is biological mother was and went to meet her. He said that he felt rejected a second time because of her "indifference" toward him.

Some lust murderers say that their life of crime came about because of the violence they had witnessed as children. For Ed Gein, his claim was that his witnessing the slaughter of farm animals was what triggered his fantasies. That does not hold much water though, because if it did, we would have to worry about thousands of 4-H members becoming serial killers. Likewise, we cannot blame the stories we read and the movies we see either. Those are just excuses that are used by killers to try to make themselves not appear as if they were monsters.

Charles Manson used to blame the reform schools he was in for "teaching him about life". You hear stories of sadistic guards all of the time and many of them were found to have credence, but does that mean that this is what triggered murderous events in the lives of these serial killers? Far too many serial killers have gone through their young lives without having been imprisoned as children.

Still, there are those who will claim that this is in fact, the case. Carl Panzram comes to mind who was by all accounts, an incorrigible delinquent.

Now let us move on and have a look at rejection by our peers when we were young. Henry Lee Lucas was painfully shy as a child and went through his young life being ridiculed because of the fact that he had an artificial eye. He went on to say that later in life, he had a general hatred for everyone because of the rejection he experienced when he was a child.

In any case, when a child becomes isolated, he begins to rely on fantasy. As the isolation becomes more severe, so too will the violent fantasies grow. More often than not, this violence will attempt to reveal itself when the appearance of at least two of the three "triads" manifests itself in the child's life. These triads do not always mean that the child will become a serial killer in life, but at the same time, there is a good chance that he "might". Now, let us take a closer look now at the Macdonald Triad.

Animal Cruelty

Animal cruelty is seen as the seed that leads to greater mayhem. It is believed that when he is torturing animals or otherwise being cruel to them, he is "practicing" for the deeds he will commit later in life. This is because for the most part, the serial killer can express his rage on the animals with little or no repercussion. In other words, he feels that he has no reason to believe that he will get into any trouble for the animal cruelty. Unfortunately, even up until now, there is very little consequence when someone is cruel to animals. Additionally, when a child is cruel to an animal, or even kills it, there is no real challenge that teaches him that what he is doing is wrong, so this in turn reinforces the belief within them that what they are doing is OK. In fact, some may even feel as if they are entitled to commit these heinous acts.

According to Robert Ressler, a world-renowned FBI agent who played a significant role in profiling serial killers, those who torture animals and set fires are likely to escalate to crimes against human beings unless the pattern is somehow broken. The torturing of animals must be looked at as a significant red flag because it is often seen as a precursor to killing a human being. That is not to say that all serial killers do this however, because there are documented cases such as with Dennis Nilsen who dearly loved his dog. Another case in point is Gary Ray Bowles, the subject of my next book. When I asked him about the McDonald Triad and whether he had ever been cruel to animals, wet the bed, or was fascinated with setting fires, he said that none of this had ever come into play at any time during his life. One factor that we have talked about in this chapter was prevalent during his adolescent years – several of his stepfathers abused him.

Pyromania

Serial killer David Berkowitz was a pyromaniac. He actually who kept meticulously detailed records of each of the fires that he had set. He had documented more than 1,400 fires throughout his lifetime. Serial killer Peter Kurten said that he loved watching a house burn while Joseph Kallinger described a fire as "heavenly pleasure". The dramatic destruction of property fulfills the same need in a serial killer that they feel when they want to destroy another person. Pyromania in fact, is often sexually stimulating for the serial killer. To the serial killer, a victim is nothing more than an object so they find it very easy to go from fire setting to killing people.

Bed Wetting

Finally, the last part of the triad is bedwetting. Bedwetting is less likely to be willfully divulged by the serial killer because of its personal nature. However, it is estimated that at least 60% of the multiple murderers that we know about have wet the bed beyond the age of 5-years-old.

It is obvious that the formative years play a significant role in the creation of a serial killer, but that is not the sole reason in every case. Many serial killers place blame on their family life as the reason for their behavior, seeking sympathy from others. It just goes to show that he is a true psychopath, blaming someone else for his actions. If having a bad childhood is the reason that a serial killer developed homicidal tendencies, then why did their siblings not also become serial killers? I myself am still not convinced that there is any one thing that is a deciding factor in whether a person becomes a serial killer. According to John Douglas (1996), serial killers are psychopathic and suffer from multiple chronic mental disorders. These people also have violent and/or abnormal social behaviors however, very few of them are actually psychotic. In fact, most people do not realize that there is even the remote possibility that a serial killer is in their midst.

According to an article written by Dr Phil, there are warning signs for the most violent of killers. These signs, he says, start during the childhood years and can give you clues. It is important to note that just because a child exhibits some of these traits, does not mean that he will become a serial killer. In fact, according to criminologist Jack Levin, most people who suffer as children will grow out of it and go on to live full, productive lives.

The ones who turn out to be serial killers are the ones who will keep repeating the same mistakes during the course of their lives. They find the transition into adulthood to be difficult and the again with the transition into middle age. When they reach a point in their lives when they feel they should be at their pinnacle, they find that they are actually sliding backwards.

He went on to say that, these people want to feel special and important. He says that they crave power, control and dominance but that they are unable to achieve their goals in any way that is accepted or is respectable. "To this end," he says, "they go out to kill, sodomize and dismember their chosen victim, and that in the end, makes them feel good about themselves."

As for the subject of our book, Joe Roy Metheny, he claims child abuse and sort of abandonment when he was young, but his mother emphatically denied that. There is also no evidence that Metheny wet his bed, set fires or was cruel to animals when he was younger, so why then, did he become a serial killer? So let us forget the triad a minute and look at what psychiatrists say that it takes to create a sociopath.

- According to studies conducted, 60% of all psychopaths had lost a parent when they were younger.
- He was deprived of love or his parents were otherwise detached when he was young.
- There was inconsistent discipline within the household. For instance, when a father is stern and the mother soft, he learns to hate the father while manipulating the mother.

- Parents are hypocritical who berate and belittle the child while in a private setting. On the other hand, when out in public they put on an image of the "happy family".

I am more inclined to look at the latter as credible proof of the possibility of a child becoming a serial killer later in life than I am with the Triad theory. In any case, there can be any number of reasons as to why someone goes out and kills a series of people. Psychopathy definitely comes into play, but my point, is that anyone of us, at any time, risks encountering a serial killer, and when he sees that we have left down our guard, he will strike.

Intelligence

Most serial killers have an IQ that falls into the bright normal range, though they will often come across to people as being above average. A serial killer will often do poorly in the school setting despite the IQ level, though there are a few who can be said to excel in school. According to FBI profilers, the serial killer will often give off the appearance of being happy; living normal lives with families and steady jobs. As a child however, their family lives have been unstable, with the serial killer often isolated from the rest of the world, or even bullied as a child.

In most cases, the serial killer is often abandoned by their fathers and will usually have a mother who is a domineering force. Again, economic standing plays no part in the make-up of the serial killer. In most but not all cases, a serial killer will suffer some sort of abuse as a child by a family member.

As a child, many serial killers will spend some time in an institution, or they will have a history of psychiatric problems. Many of those with serial killer traits become interested in voyeurism and fetishism from an early age. Many are also interested in sado-masochistic pornography and engage in sado-masochistic sex. Those falling into the serial killer category come from a group of people with a high rate of suicide.

Now let us look at geography. As far as the United States is concerned, California is home to the largest number of serial killers and serial homicide cases. Because of the body counts involved, these serial killers are more notorious than others are. In fact, there have been times when California had several serial murder cases going at the same time. Serial killers like Rodney Alcala, the so-called "Dating Game Killer" were able to fly under
the radar for so long because when police were getting closer to him, he fled to New York, changing his name at the same time, where he also preyed on women. Alcala was working as a camp counselor when girls from the camp recognized him from a wanted poster they spotted in a post office. The police were called and he was finally arrested

and brought to justice.

Statistically, 65% of the serial killer's victims will be female. While there are a number of known serial killers all over the world, the majority originate in the United States. In fact, somewhere around 72% of all known serial murderers are located in the U.S. at the time of publication. England comes in second place, with the dubious honor of claiming 4% of the serial killer population. The remainder comes from the rest of the world. There is little doubt however that the United States is king when it comes to producing these psychopaths.

"The only thing they can get me for is running a funeral parlor without a license."
– John Wayne Gacy

4 – TONI INGRASSIA

Toni Lynn Ingrassia, Metheny's first known victim, was also unknown to police until Metheny was finally captured and confessed to the crime. She disappeared in November of 1993, when the weather had turned cold.

Toni, whose body was found in February 1994, was dumped on the shoulder of I-95 at the Caton Avenue ramp, near where Metheny was employed at Joe Stein and Sons.

Toni's murder investigation would long be remembered as one that was botched by the Maryland Transportation Authority Police. In their defense, it was only the second murder investigation that fell into the jurisdiction of the agency since it had been created, but they still could have called in help, and perhaps Metheny might have been brought to justice before anyone else was killed.

That's really not a fair statement perhaps, but the agency believed that what they had was a murder committed by someone who was passing through. That's still no excuse for the haphazard way the evidence was collected and handled.

Had Metheny not confessed to killing the woman, her murder would still be unsolved to this day.

Toni was described by her father as "a good girl" who had a drug problem. Attempts to contact Toni's father for the purposes of this book failed, in that at the very least, he refused to respond to letters sent asking for an interview. Many hours of research has been conducted in attempt to learn more about Toni Lynn, but the best information found was that she had a relatively minor arrest record which consisted only three separate incidents – all drug possession charges. The first two were disposed of by her appearance in court. The third had been abated due to her murder.

No one knows how she initially came into contact with Metheny. Perhaps Metheny had met her in the Borderline Bar and Restaurant like he had done with Magaziner, on the pretense of using drugs and getting high. Also, no one, including Metheny himself, knows why he snapped and began his string of murders with her when there was really no indication that he would ever kill anyone. That is of course, unless you believe his story that it was his ex taking off with his son that caused him to snap.

It stands to reason that Toni was someone that

Metheny had known from the drug scene. In Southwest Baltimore, as with any other city, people in the underground drug community all seem to know one another, or at the very least, KNOW OF one another. Metheny states that it was winter time when he killed her, and court records show that she was released on bail from her last drug charge on January 5, 1994. That said, she disappeared and was subsequently murder sometime soon thereafter. According to Metheny, he does not remember the exact date, though it is likely that he does.

What probably happened was that Toni was looking to get high, and as many of those who make up the drug-user population in Baltimore are, she was perhaps looking for a place to crash for the night. It is now known that Metheny had taken his victim's to "his place", which consisted of an unused truck trailer that was on the Stein and Sons property. Metheny had converted it into his living quarters under an arrangement that he had with Joseph Stein, Sr. whereas Metheny would live in the trailer and in turn, keep an eye on the pallet company property.

When she encountered Metheny, perhaps she let him know that she needed a place to stay by asking if he knew of a place she could crash for the night, or perhaps he even offered it from the beginning. In any case, she ended up there, and she ended up dead. Her body then dumped on I-95 at Caton Avenue.

"When this monster entered my brain, I will never know, but it is here to stay. How does one cure himself? I can't stop it, the monster goes on, and hurts me as well as society. Maybe you can stop him. I can't." – **Dennis Rader**

5 – CATHY MAGAZINER, RANDALL PIKER AND RANDY BREWER

According to the timeline, Cathy Ann Magaziner is the second victim that Metheny had murdered and could be verified. Little information is known about Ms Magaziner. A search of court records show her birth date as being November 21, 1957. She didn't appear in Maryland's judicial system for the first time until 1991, making her around 34-years-old the first time she had ever gotten in trouble with the law.

A search on the internet turned up very little information as well, but there are some clues that she had perhaps relocated here from another state, most likely Mississippi. Still, her arrest records give the most information, and also gives a clue as to why police initially thought Metheny was targeting prostitutes.

Her arrest record indicates that most of the

charges brought against her were relatively minor and included not only charges of loitering for the purposes of prostitution, but drug possession and open container charges as well. Additionally, there were several charges for theft of less than $300.00 value, likely for shoplifting.

According to Metheny, he had met Magaziner on a July night in 1994, most likely in the vicinity of the Borderline Bar and Restaurant, his "hang out" of choice. He then lured her to his trailer located in the parking lot of the Joe Stein and Son Pallet Company located on James Street in the Baltimore Suburb of Arbutus. Most like his con was that they were going back to his trailer to use drugs.

Metheny says that he and Magaziner had sex while she was partially clothed. It is unknown as to whether or not the sex was consensual. He said that they had been in the trailer for about an hour before he strangled her to death.

After she was dead, he said that he removed the rest of her clothing and buried her in a shallow grave, about two feet deep, in the wooded area surrounding the pallet company property. He then said that he returned to the grave about six months later, dug up the body and removed the head, throwing it in the trash. According to official court documents, the trash that her head ended up in was later transported to Oxford, Pennsylvania.

When making his confession, Metheny described

Magaziner as being "a little on the tall side" with a thin build and brown hair. According to police, his details were vague, and initial attempts to recover the body had failed because Metheny gave them the wrong location. The police employed the use of cadaver dogs, but the indicated the wrong location as well, probably because of rain drainage spreading the scent.

At some point, Detective Homer Pennington of the Baltimore City Police Department's Homicide Unit obtained a writ to remove Metheny from jail. He then took Metheny to the pallet company grounds so that he could show police exactly where he had buried the body. Metheny also pointed out where he had buried the victim's belongings, but police never did recover the woman's clothing or purse.

During questioning, police asked Metheny why he killed the woman. Metheny replied, "I don't know. Sense of power. Vulnerable. I dreaded, just I got very… got a rush out of it, got a high out of it. Call it what you want. I had no real excuse why other than I like to do it."

Later on, after the trial and sentencing, Metheny would claim that he had had sex with the dead bodies of his victims. He also mad other outrageous claims that were never proven according to police, but Metheny himself says that he is telling the truth.

It's hard to say what led to the murders of Randy Piker and Randall Brewer in August 1995, except for

Joe himself and the two men. What is known, is that though he was charged with their murders, a jury found him not guilty, and going so far as to state that they believed another man was the actual culprit. In the end however, Metheny later admitted that he was in fact the one that murdered the two men.

At some point, Metheny had gone to an area known as "Tent City" under the Patapsco River bridge, accessible from Patapsco Avenue near Potee Street. The area has long since been cleared out, but it was once a thriving community of homeless men. A lawless community where it was more or less every man for himself and violence was the theme of each and every day.

Whatever way he encountered these two men, whom he himself claims were sleeping and bothering no one until he woke them. He ostensibly woke them on the pretext of finding out where his ex "ol' lady" was, even going so far as to make claims that she had recently been there getting high with the two men. Whatever the exchange ultimately was between the three, the two Randy's ended up back on the dirty mattress that they had been sleeping on, the difference now however, was that they were dead, having been bludgeoned and hacked with an old ax that Metheny had found nearby.

According to Metheny, he had gone to look for his ex-wife and her new man, with the intention of killing them.

He said that he went to the homeless camp, known as "Tent City" to find them. He said that he never found his ex and her boyfriend, but that he did learn from the two homeless men that they had gotten high with at least the ex-wife.

He said that when he initially found the two men, they had been sleeping on an old mattress under the Patapsco River bridge on Patapsco Avenue. He said that he killed the two men by hitting them about the head and body with an old ax that he found nearby. He said that when he left, they were on the mattress, one on top of the other.

Metheny also claims that he had killed two "crack whores" that day, plus an old black man who was fishing and simply ended up being in the wrong place at the wrong time and Metheny believed that the man had witnessed him killing the second woman.

In news articles of the *Baltimore Sun*, the police said that Metheny had told them that he killed the three and threw them into the Patapsco River, weighing their bodies down with large rocks. Extensive searches of the area turned up nothing, and police said that they could not match the descriptions Metheny gave them with any known missing persons.

After an exhaustive search for information about Piker and Brewer, the only thing that could be found was that they both had minor arrest records, mostly involving drug possession and some theft charges. He said that he went to the homeless camp, known as "Tent City" to find them. He said that he never found his ex and her boyfriend, but that he did learn from the two homeless men that they had gotten high with at least the ex-wife.

He said that when he initially found the two men, they had been sleeping on an old mattress under the Patapsco River bridge on Patapsco Avenue. He said that he killed the two men by hitting them about the head and body with an old ax that he found nearby. He said that when he left, they were on the mattress, one on top of the other.

Metheny also claims that he had killed two "crack whores" that day, plus an old black man who was fishing and simply ended up being in the wrong place at the wrong time and Metheny believed that the man had witnessed him killing the second woman.

In news articles of the *Baltimore Sun*, the police said that Metheny had told them that he killed the three and threw them into the Patapsco River, weighing their bodies down with large rocks. Extensive searches of the area turned up nothing, and police said that they could not match the descriptions Metheny gave them with any known missing persons.

After an exhaustive search for information about Piker and Brewer, the only thing that could be found was that they both had minor arrest records, mostly involving drug possession and some theft charges

Metheny was actually arrested and charged with murdering Piker and Brewer in 1995 and was acquitted in July of 1996. According to court records, the Court concluded that there was insufficient evidence to convict him of the double-murder. Jurors that sat on the trial indicated that they believed another man committed the murders based on the testimony and evidence that they heard.

Metheny spent the entire time after his arrest in jail awaiting trial on the murder charges. When he was acquitted, he was released from jail and talked his boss, Joe Stein into giving him his job back.

After his arrest for the murder of Kimberly Spicer (next chapter), Metheny would admit that it was in fact him that murdered the two men at the homeless camp in August 1995.

"May your wife and children get raped, right in the ass! – **Aileen Wuornos**

6 KIM SPICER AND RITA KEMPER

Kimberly Lynn Spicer was reported missing by her mother on November 11, 1996. She had actually went missing two weeks before that, making her probable murder date during the last week of October, 1996. She was found a little over a month later, under a semi-truck trailer on the property of the Joe Stein and Son Pallet Company property. Her body had been covered with pallets to hide it, but you can be sure that the pallets were not covering the rank odor of decay. While the smell probably had been lessened due to the cold weather, there must have still been the tell tale signs of a rotting body around, whatever it was. It was a series of unfortunate events that led Kim right into Joe's hands that fateful night. It took some time for the police to uncover all of the details, but when they did, they painted a clear picture of just what happened.

According to Kim's mother, she and Kim had

gotten into one of their many arguments on the day that she went missing. It would seem that Kim and Joe had known each other on some level. At the very least, they knew one another from the Southwest Baltimore drug scene. Kim had once told her sister, Connie Snow, that she felt sorry for the big man that they called Tiny.

Details were undisclosed about what the argument was over between Kim and her mother, but it is known that Kim's mother, Kathy Price was upset over the death of her brother, who had died in an abandoned house on Wilkens Avenue due to a heroin overdose. Price said that she and Kim had argued before, and that Kim would leave for awhile, but that she had always come back. She stated that on that particular night however, Kim must have run into Metheny on the "Boulevard", meaning Washington Boulevard.

In any case, Kim stormed out of the house that night, never to return. A unidentified witness, who had been at Uncle Walt's bar, located in the 2300 block of Washington Boulevard in the Morrell Park area of the city, said that Kim had approached her multiple times that night asking if she could spend the night at her house. The woman said that she denied Kim's request because she didn't know her that well.

A little while later, she said that she had seen Kim outside of the bar, talking to "Tiny". The woman then said that she and a friend had left the bar a little while later and had given Joe Metheny and Kimberly a ride to the Joe Stein and Sons Pallet Company. Spicer was never to be seen again. What actually happened once the pair arrived at Metheny's trailer is unknown, except that Kim's body would be found a little over a month later, strangled and stabbed to death.

Before Kim's body was ever found however, Metheny had yet another victim, except this one would live to tell the tale of just how much of a monster Joe Metheny was and probably still is.

Metheny's fall had already started, but he didn't know it yet. His first fatal mistake was in trying to enlist the help of a coworker to get rid of Kimberly Spicer's body. Had he kept his mouth shut, it's highly likely she may never have been found.

The second fatal mistake of Metheny was his encounter with 37-year-old Rita Kemper. It was on December 8, 1996 when Metheny lured Rita Jean Kemper to his trailer. This was only about a week before police found the body of Kimberly Spicer a mere 10 feet away from the truck trailer that Metheny called his home.

The two went to his trailer that night intending to share drugs. Kemper explained in court that the two had developed a friendship the previous Fall, sharing cocaine together are different times, but that they had never had a sexual relationship.

Once in the trailer, Metheny ordered Kemper to take her clothes off but she refused to do so. He struck her twice but she managed to escape through the trailer door. Metheny then chased after the woman and caught her, bringing her back into the trailer. Kemper then said that she screamed and that Metheny simply laughed at her, telling her that nop one could hear her so she could scream all she wanted.

"Whatever Tiny wanted to do that night, he was going to do," she told the court. She went on to say that she knew he wasn't going to let her out of that trailer alive because he said, "I'm going to kill you and bury you in the woods with the other girls." Kemper said she had no intention of dying without putting up a fight.

According to Metheny's account of the crimes he committed that night, he turned away for a split second, and that was his mistake. He said that he had no more than turned than she was up and out of the trailer and running through the pallet company lot. He said "There were stacks of pallets all over the place and against the perimeter fence. The fence was about 8-feet high with barbed wire at the top. The stacks of pallets were about 10-feet high. That bitch scaled that stack of pallets like she was a monkey and jumped over the fence. She ran down to the main street and flagged some asshole down who took her to call the police."

Metheny's recount of the nights events do not match what he told police when he was arrested, nor does the account accurately match how he was arrested. The essence of the story was true however. He would lead people to believe that police came that night and arrested him, however, the reality was that he was arrested, along with his boss Joe Stein, Sr. as he left a Christmas party that they were attending together on December 15, 1996. He would also spin stories that he gave the police the run-around while they were looking for the bodies of his victims, including Spicer's body. That simply is not true, as the police had located Spicer's remains shortly after arresting Metheny. Metheny's boss, Joe Stein, Sr. had been charged as an accessory because they believed that he had helped Metheny to dispose of evidence. It is unclear as to whether or not he was convicted of that crime since the only charge that could be found was his arrest on the charges of premeditated murder which were not prosecuted.

It is more likely that the State never prosecuted Stein on any of the charges they lodged at the request of the FBI, who had their own agenda involving the elder Stein.

"It wasn't as dark and scary as it sounds. I had a lot of fun...killing somebody's a funny experience." – **Albert DeSalvo**

7 COURT

Metheny was actually charged for the murders of Randall Piker and Randy Brewer right around the time that they were murdered. While he did spend a few months in jail awaiting trial, he was acquitted of the crimes and the jury on the case even indicated to the judge that they believed the murders were committed by another man.

Metheny would later admit that he had murdered the men using an ax, although he embellished the story a bit and made it sound as if he had chopped the men up into pieces.

His next appearance in court was for the crimes he committed against Rita Kemper. Metheny's attorneys would claim throughout the trial that Kemper's claims had been exaggerated and that this was simply a case of a prostitute looking for attention. In fact, some of the jurors even stated that they had a hard time believing Kemper's story because of the fact that she had shared drugs with Metheny and was a known prostitute.

Nonetheless, Metheny was found guilty and sentencing was scheduled for a later date pending a presentencing investigation. Metheny faced as many as 50-years in prison for the crimes he had committed.

When the sentencing phase of the trial came around, Metheny was given the maximum penalty of 50-years. Lawyers were disappointed and in fact had been expecting Judge John N. Prevas to impose a sentence of five to ten years. Lawyers told the press that they believed that Prevas had actually considered the pending murder charges when imposing sentence.

Prevas said during sentencing, "I wouldn't wish being in the trailer that night with Mr. Metheny on anyone. A horrible thing has happened to Ms. Kemper." He went on to say that he didn't even consider the pending murder charges, but that he based the sentencing strictly on the kidnapping and attempted rape of Ms. Kemper as well as Metheny's previous record.

Metheny never did stand trial for the charges against him involving the murder of Toni Lynn Ingrassia. Prosecutors said that they simply did not have enough evidence to prove that he did in fact kill her. Also, they were certain that they were going to get convictions on him for the Spicer and Magaziner murders.

Metheny's next trial was for the murder of Cathy Ann Magaziner. After hearing the evidence which included a taped confession, jurors spent two hours deliberating before finally coming back with a verdict of guilty.

During the trial, Metheny stated that the words "I'm sorry" would never come out of his mouth because they would be a lie. He also said that he had enjoyed killing the woman and was prepared to accept death as his penalty for the crime. He went on to say that he would let God judge and send him to Hell for all eternity.

Metheny's attorneys had argued all along that Metheny's case did not qualify for the death penalty. Regardless of that fact, Metheny was indeed given the death penalty for his crimes against Magaziner. His next trial would be for the murder of Kimberly Spicer.

In that trial, Metheny was once again found guilty and sentenced to life in prison without the possibility of parole. But that was not to be the end of his trials. In 2000, lawyers successfully argued that the death penalty was not applicable to the murder of Cathy Ann Magaziner because the case did not support the special circumstances required in the State of Maryland to support a death verdict.

The appeals court agreed with the attorneys and commuted the sentence from death to life without parole.

The story of Joe Roy Metheny is not over though. To this day, Metheny claims that the reason police were unable to find other bodies is because he cannibalized them.

According to his story, he had open a pit beef/pork stand on the grounds of the pallet company on the weekends. This part of the story has been confirmed as true by friends and acquaintances of Joe Metheny. At this sandwich stand, he says that he ground up the flesh from some of his victims and then mixed it in with the regular meat.

There are several people, who refused to be identified, that confirmed this part of his story, and claim that they would never buy sandwich's from his stand because they "didn't know what was in them". Still others say that he was making this claim simply to sensationalize the story even more.

Baltimore City Police say that Metheny's claims are outrageous and that there is absolutely no evidence to support his claims.

Metheny says: "So the next time you're riding down the road and you happen to see an open pit beef stand, that you've never seen before, make sure you think about this story before you take a bite of that sandwich. Sometimes you never know who you may be eating. Ha! Ha!"

8 RESOURCES

I gathered information for this story from the following sources:

1. Baltimore Sun
2. Baltimore City Circuit Court
3. Baltimore County Circuit Court
4. Murderpedia.com
5. Maryland Judiciary Case Search

"Even when she was dead, she was still bitching at me. I couldn't get her to shut up!" **– Edmund Kemper**

ABOUT THE AUTHOR

J.R. Brand (1965) was born in Baltimore, Maryland. He started writing for his own pleasure while in high school. John has been an internet entrepreneur for more than fourteen years. He began writing content for his own websites, and as his skills improved, he began writing content for websites like GMC.com, Loan.com and dozens of others.

"Murder in Southwest Baltimore – Joe Roy Metheny is the first book published by J.R. Brand, a short book of just over 11,000 words. His first love in writing however is fiction and he expects to release his first full-length novel in November 2015

www.ingramcontent.com/pod-product-compliance
Lightning Source LLC
Chambersburg PA
CBHW071932020426
42331CB00010B/2838